My Mouth

By Lloyd G. Douglas

Children's Press®
A Division of Scholastic Inc.
New York / Toronto / London / Auckland / Sydney
Mexico City / New Delhi / Hong Kong
Danbury, Connecticut

Photo Credits: Cover © Raoul Minsart/Corbis; p. 5 © Photodisc/Getty Images; p. 7 © Anthony Nex/Corbis; p. 9 © LWA-Dann Tardif/Corbis; pp. 11, 21 (top left) © Henry Feather/Corbis; pp. 13, 21 (top right) © Norbert Schaefer/Corbis; pp. 15, 21 (bottom left) © Tom & Dee Ann McCarthy/Corbis; p. 17 © Richard Hutchings/Corbis; pp. 19, 21 (bottom right) © Ed Bock/Corbis
Contributing Editor: Shira Laskin
Book Design: Michael de Guzman

Library of Congress Cataloging-in-Publication Data

Douglas, Lloyd G.
    My mouth / by Lloyd G. Douglas.
    p. cm.—(My body)
    Includes index.
    Summary: Simple text introduces the functions of the human mouth, as well as how dentists keep our teeth healthy.
    ISBN 0-516-24061-7 (lib. bdg.) — ISBN 0-516-22131-0 (pbk.)
    1. Mouth—Juvenile literature. [1. Mouth.] I. Title.

QM306.D68 2004
612.3'1—dc22

2003012300

Contents

I have a mouth.

Inside my mouth, I have
a **tongue** and teeth.

Mouths help us do
many things.

We use our mouths to eat.

Our teeth help us **chew** food.

They break the food into small pieces.

We use our tongues to taste food.

Ice cream tastes sweet.

We use our mouths to talk, too.

We move our mouths to say words.

13

Our mouths also help
us breathe.

They help us get air into
and out of our bodies.

We can blow air
into **balloons**.

15

We use **toothbrushes** and **toothpaste** to keep our mouths clean.

We also go to the **dentist**.

Dentists help us keep our mouths healthy.

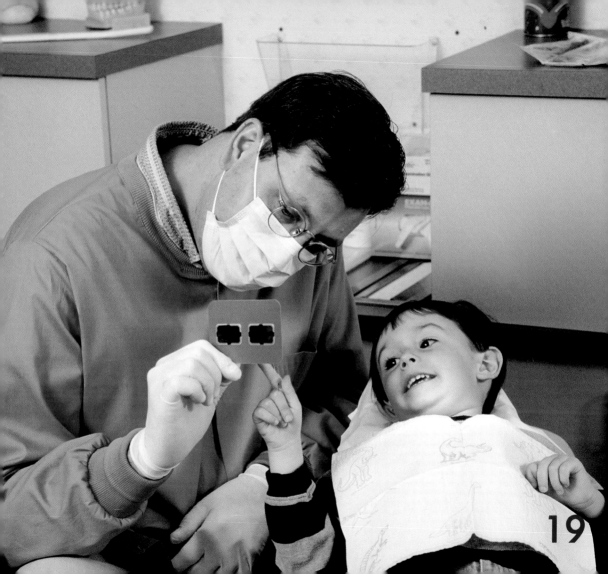

19

Mouths are very **useful** parts of our bodies.

New Words

balloons (buh-**loonz**) small bags made of thin rubber that are blown up and used as decoration

chew (**choo**) to break food into small pieces with your teeth

dentist (**dent**-uhst) a doctor who takes care of people's teeth and gums and helps to keep them healthy

tongue (**tuhng**) the movable muscle in your mouth that is used for tasting, swallowing, and talking

toothbrushes (**tooth**-bruhsh-uhz) small brushes used to clean teeth

toothpaste (**tooth**-payst) a paste that is put on toothbrushes and used to clean the teeth

useful (**yooss**-fuhl) something that is helpful and can be used a lot

To Find Out More

Books
Animal Mouths
by David M. Schwartz
Creative Teaching Press

Mouths and Teeth
by Elizabeth Miles
Heinemann Library

Web Site
ADHA: Kids Site
http://www.adha.org/kidstuff/index.html
Learn about the mouth and play games on this Web site.

Index

About the Author
Lloyd G. Douglas has written many books for children.

Reading Consultants
Kris Flynn, Coordinator, Small School District Literacy, The San Diego County Office of Education

Shelly Forys, Certified Reading Recovery Specialist, W.J. Zahnow Elementary School, Waterloo, IL

Paulette Mansell, Certified Reading Recovery Specialist, and Early Literacy Consultant, TX